SILVER SHADOW STRIKES OUT

Philip Ardagh
Steve Cole

Pictures by
Bill Ledger

OXFORD
UNIVERSITY PRESS

OXFORD
UNIVERSITY PRESS

Great Clarendon Street, Oxford, OX2 6DP,
United Kingdom

Oxford University Press is a department of the University of Oxford.
It furthers the University's objective of excellence in research, scholarship,
and education by publishing worldwide. Oxford is a registered trade mark of
Oxford University Press in the UK and in certain other countries

British Library Cataloguing in Publication Data
Data available

9780192776068

1 3 5 7 9 10 8 6 4 2

Paper used in the production of this book is a natural, recyclable product
made from wood grown in sustainable forests. The manufacturing process conforms
to the environmental regulations of the country of origin.
Printed in China

Acknowledgements
Illustrations by Bill Ledger
Activities by Rachel Russ
Design by James W Hunter
Photo assets supplied by shutterstock.com, cgtrader.com, turbosquid.com.

CONTENTS

Helping your child to read

Before they start

- Talk about the back cover blurb. Ask your child whether they think Ben will defeat Silver Shadow.
- Look at the front cover. Talk about who Silver Shadow could be.

During reading

- Let your child read at their own pace – don't worry if it's slow. They could read silently, or read to you out loud.
- Help them to work out words they don't know by saying each sound out loud and then blending them to say the word, e.g. *c-r-ow-d-ed*, *crowded*.
- If your child still struggles with a word, just tell them the word and move on.
- Give them lots of praise for good reading!

After reading

- Look at pages 29 and 55 for some fun activities.

SILVER SHADOW

Philip Ardagh

Pictures by
Bill Ledger

In this story ...

Ben
(**SPRINT**)

Ben is super fast! He can run faster than a
racing car. Once, he ran five times round
the school grounds in under ten seconds.

Mrs Molten
(**TEACHER**)

Slink
(**COMBAT CAT**)

1
SLINK IS MISSING

Slink had gone missing.

When most cats go missing, their owners shout, "**Here, puss!**" They shake boxes of kitty treats ...

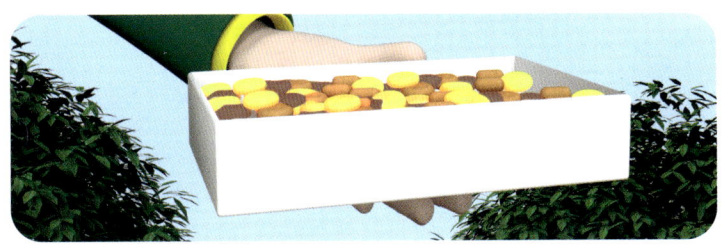

... and put up **LOST CAT** posters.

When Slink disappeared, there was **PANIC**. Why? Because Slink was no ordinary cat. He helped the Head run Hero Academy.

Mrs Molten was in her office. She sent a message asking Ben to come and see her. She hardly had time to lean back in her chair before Ben appeared.

"We have a problem," said Mrs Molten. **"Slink is missing!** The tracker in his collar is sending out a signal, but the signal is weak. We have to find him before the signal stops and we can't track him any more."

Mrs Molten handed Ben a wrist-watch tracker, which picked up the signal from Slink's collar. "Put it on and follow the red dot," she said.

2

TRACKING SLINK

Lexis City was noisy and crowded. However, everyone was busy listening to music, talking on their phones or dashing into shops. They didn't even look at Ben as he CHARGED past.

Every so often, Ben stopped to look at the tracker to check he was going the right way.

Once, he got very close to Slink, but the signal quickly began to fade.

Then it disappeared altogether.

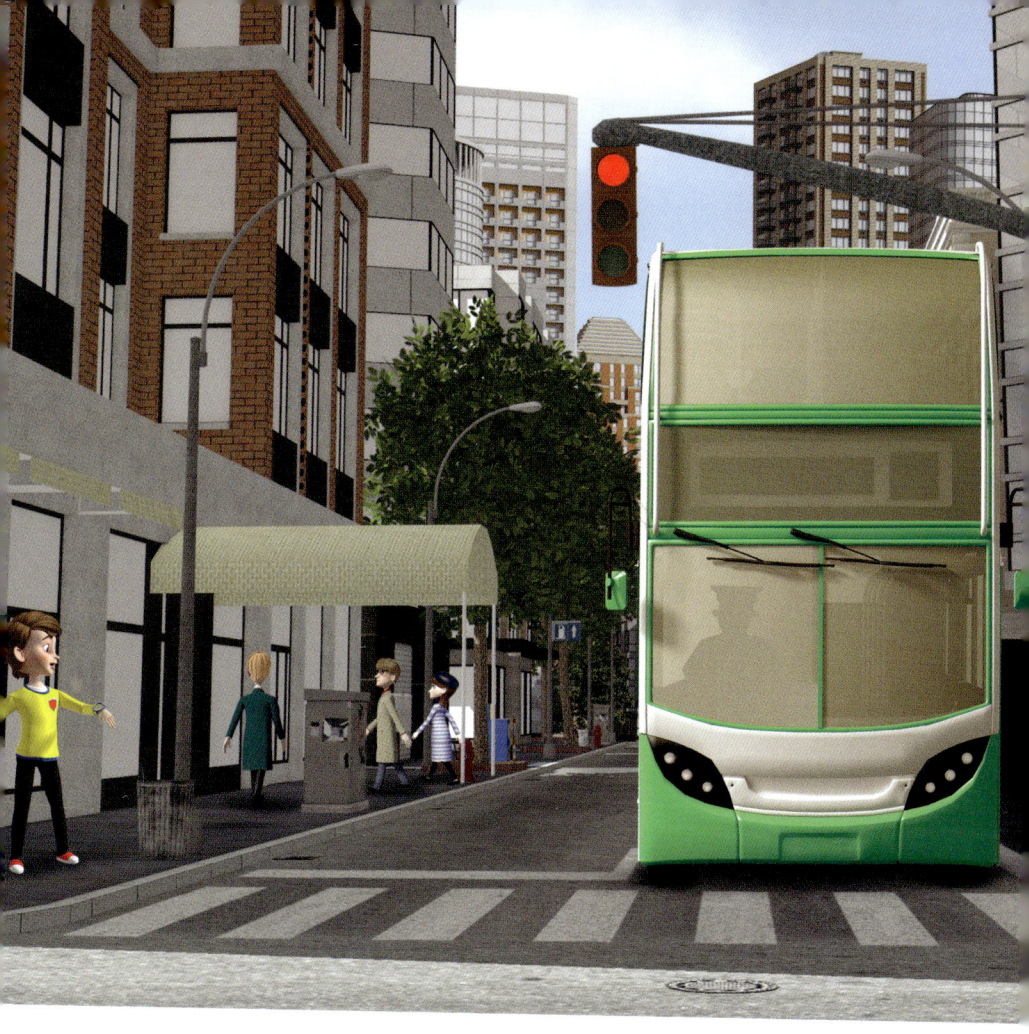

Ben kept running, hoping the signal would come back. He reached a set of traffic lights.

Suddenly, the signal came back. Apparently Slink was right next to him! **How? Where?**

The signal started to move as the bus next to Ben set off. Slink must be on board! Ben dashed ahead of the bus to the next stop. When the bus pulled up, Ben jumped on and bought a ticket.

Bus stop

Ben looked around. There was Slink, asleep on a sweet, old lady's lap. He had a contented smile on his face. There was a knitting bag at the lady's feet. She was busy knitting what looked like a **life-sized** woolly cat!

3

ROCKET-POWERED ROLLER SKATES

Ben looked at the lady more closely. His blood ran cold. This 'sweet, old lady' was none other than **SILVER SHADOW**! She was number four on Police Commissioner Jordan's Most Wanted Villain list! Somehow she must have tricked Slink and taken him prisoner!

SILVER SHADOW

Catchphrase: I'll knit you into knots!

Hobbies: knitting, driving speedboats.

Likes: boiled sweets, burglary.

Dislikes: knots in her wool, noise, losing her false teeth.

Beware! Don't let this villain's appearance fool you. She likes nothing better than robbing banks and stealing other people's inventions. She boasts about the fact that she often gets out of jail by using her sewing skills to pick the locks of the prison doors.

Silver Shadow sensed Ben watching her.
She slipped still-snoring Slink into her
knitting bag. When she stood up, Ben
spotted that she
was wearing
rocket-powered
roller skates!

Before Ben knew what was happening,
Silver Shadow **zoomed** down the aisle and
jumped off the bus at the next stop. Ben
spun into his superhero costume
and **darted** off after her.
Silver Shadow was no
match for Sprint!

Silver Shadow reached into her knitting bag and began to lob, roll and throw things at Sprint. These included: **balls of wool, boiled sweets, a box of Cat Snax** and **a set of false teeth.** Sprint managed to catch the Cat Snax and dodge the rest.

Suddenly, Silver Shadow *SPED* down an alleyway. Sprint *CHASED* her. He could see Slink's head poking out of the top of the knitting bag. He was still sleeping, blissfully unaware of what was happening.

The alley was a dead end. Silver Shadow had reached a high brick wall. She bent down and pushed a button on her rocket-powered roller skates. They became **jet boots** instead!

"Think you can catch me, you pesky hero?" she screeched. "**HA!**"

She began to hover in the air, ready to take Slink over the wall and out of reach.

Sprint was still holding the box of Cat Snax which Silver Shadow had thrown at him. Now he threw it back. The box went spinning through the air. It knocked the knitting bag right out of Silver Shadow's hands!

Sprint **darted** over and scooped up
the bag and the sleepy cat.

Silver Shadow was FURIOUS. She
rocketed up over the wall and away.
Her plan had been ruined!

4
MISSION ACCOMPLISHED

Back at the academy, Ben told Mrs Molten about Silver Shadow's dastardly plan. "She caught Slink using some special cat biscuits to make him sleepy," Ben explained.

Slink gave an embarrassed **meow**. He could never resist cat biscuits.

"I found these plans in Silver Shadow's bag," said Ben. "She was going to build a robot cat just like Slink."

"What on earth for?" asked Mrs Molten.

BLUEPRINTS

"Silver Shadow was knitting a 'Slink coat'
to cover the robot," Ben said. "She wanted
to swap Slink for the robot cat and send
it here to find out all our **secrets!**"

"Except **YOU** managed to stop her," said
Mrs Molten. "Well done, Ben!"

Ben glowed with pride, and Slink let him rub the space between his ears, which was a very rare honour indeed.

MISSION ACCOMPLISHED!

purrrr

purrrr

AFTER READING ACTIVITIES

QUICK QUIZ

See how fast you can answer these questions!
Look back at the story if you can't remember.

1) Who is missing at the beginning of the story?

2) What does Silver Shadow wear on her feet?

3) What does Ben throw to knock the knitting bag out of Silver Shadow's hands?

THINK ABOUT IT!

Do you think Silver Shadow is a surprising villain? Why?

IMAGINE IT

Which things does Silver Shadow take out of her knitting bag and throw at Ben?

29

Answers: 1) Slink;
2) rocket-powered roller skates;
3) a box of Cat Snax.

SILVER SHADOW STRIKES AGAIN

Steve Cole

Pictures by
Bill Ledger

In this story ...

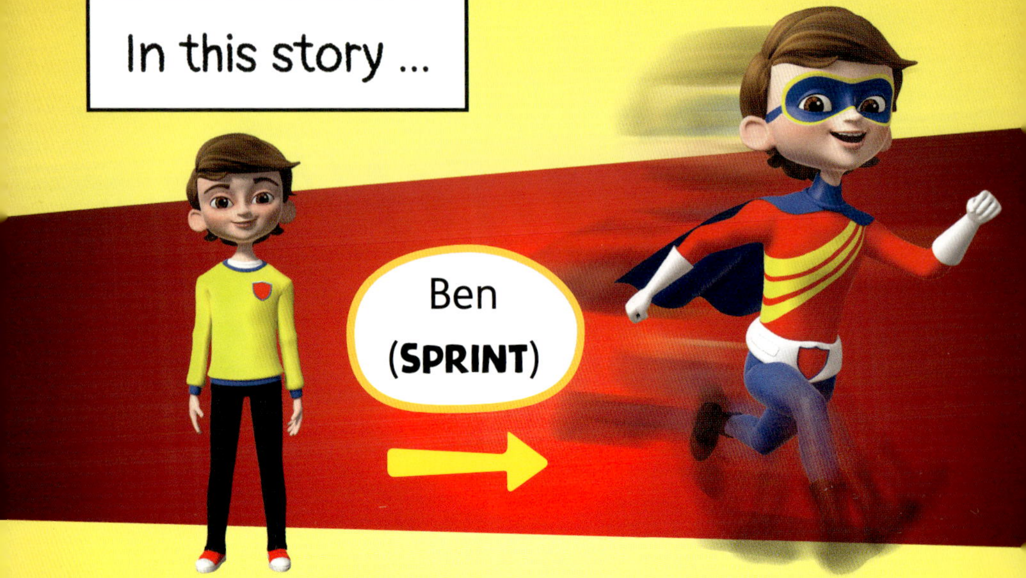

Ben
(**SPRINT**)

Ben is super fast! He can run faster than a racing car. He once ran around Hero Academy so fast he created a tornado.

Mrs Molten
(**TEACHER**)

1
A SPEEDY MISSION

"Attention, class!" Mrs Molten said. "Today we will test the strength of some new and unusual materials."

"Cool!" said Ben. He loved Mrs Molten's lessons. There were always interesting experiments to do, although you never knew quite what would happen.

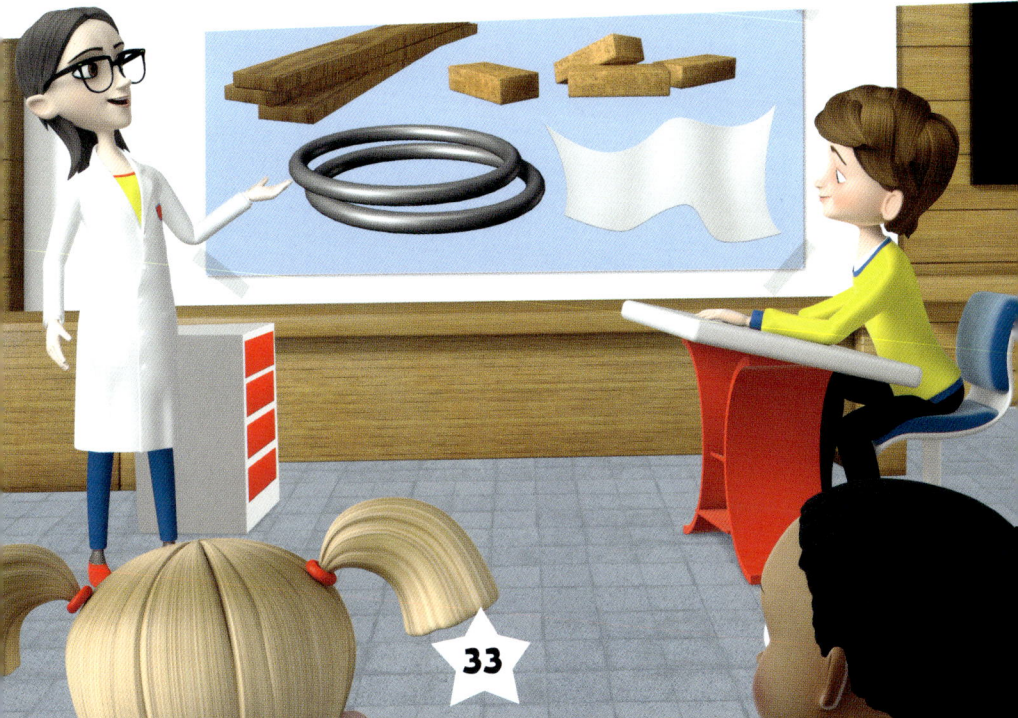

"Oh no!" groaned Mrs Molten as she searched in a drawer. "I forgot the **Super Stretchy Elastic**."

"What's that?" asked Ben.

"It's a top-secret, extra-strong material invented by my friend, Professor Bounce," Mrs Molten explained. "He made me a batch for testing, but I forgot to pick it up."

"Can I help?" asked Ben.

"Would you collect the **Super Stretchy Elastic** from Professor Bounce's workshop, please?" asked Mrs Molten.

"Of course!" Ben said, spinning into his superhero costume and becoming Sprint.

Mrs Molten handed him the address. "It shouldn't take more than ten minutes."

"I'll do it in five minutes!" cried Sprint. In a blur of speed, he ran out of the classroom.

Sprint **raced** through the streets of Lexis City. He loved to feel the air on his face as he ran. It kept him cool as the sun beat down.

Soon, he reached Professor Bounce's workshop. It had wooden walls and diamond-shaped windows.

Sprint saw someone outside the workshop's front door. It was a woman wearing a thick coat, despite the heat. She was pushing on the door with all her strength.

Sprint GULPED. It looked as though she was trying to break in!

2
THE BEST WAY IN

Sprint was about to run to the police station and report the woman when she suddenly turned to him. She was an old lady with pinky-purple hair and glasses. Sprint had a feeling he had seen her before.

"I didn't see you there, dear," said the old lady. "I'm Sylvia Shadow, Professor Bounce's housekeeper."

Sprint smiled. He was glad he hadn't gone to the police.

"I've just come to pick up a package from Professor Bounce," he explained.

"He's not here at the moment." Sylvia's eyes filled with tears. "Actually, I'm worried I'll lose my job."

"Why?" asked Sprint. "What's happened?"

"I'm here to clean the workshop, but I've lost my keys," Sylvia replied. "Professor Bounce will be **FURIOUS** that I've lost them. He keeps lots of secret inventions inside, you see. It would be awful if someone stole them."

"My teacher sent me to collect one of them," said Sprint.

"Then we both need to get inside." Sylvia sniffed. "Let me try the door again."

Before Sprint could say anything, the old lady leaned against the door and pushed hard. **CRUNCH!** The door broke off its hinges!

"*Oopsie!*" Sylvia smiled. "I don't know my own strength."

THE ANTI-INTRUDER SYSTEM

Sylvia moved to one side to let Sprint go in first.

Sprint stepped into the hallway. He saw a parcel addressed to Mrs Molten leaning against the wall.

"The **Super Stretchy Elastic!**" Sprint thought.

To Mrs Molten

Suddenly, something large and metallic clanked into the hallway. It looked like a robot dog. When it saw Sprint, its eyes glowed red and it showed its SPIKY teeth.

"It's the guard dog!" cried Sylvia. "I'm afraid it thinks you broke in!"

"**Me?**" Sprint began.

"Well, you were the first one inside," she replied.

With a mechanical SNARL, the robot guard dog charged.

Sprint turned and ran.

The guard dog chased him around the garden. Its metal jaws SNAPPED open and shut, trying to grab Sprint's cape.

"This is all a mistake!" Sprint panted. "Professor Bounce knows my teacher."

Sprint did several laps around a flowerbed, trying to escape from the guard dog.

"Sylvia, help!" Sprint cried. "Can you turn it off?"

"No, dear. I can't," she replied from the doorway. "Look out for the nets! They're also part of Professor Bounce's anti-intruder system."

Sprint stared in horror as two big nets, like monstrous birds, came flapping towards him.

4

SILVER SHADOW

Sprint ran *faster* and *faster*, ducking as the nets **SWOOPED** over his head. The guard dog barked. Smoke puffed out of its metal nostrils.

"**Keep going!**" called Sylvia. "The guard dog's overheating!"

Just then ... **BOOM!** Sparks flew out of the robot guard dog and bits fell off it. Then it stopped.

Sprint ran past the broken dog as one of the flying nets dived towards him. The net trapped the dog instead. He couldn't avoid the second net, however. It caught him, pinning him to the ground.

"Well done. Thanks to you, I don't have to worry about the anti-intruder system." Sylvia smiled nastily. "Now I can steal Professor Bounce's inventions."

Sprint's mouth fell open. "I thought you were Professor Bounce's housekeeper?"

"**Fooled you!**" Sylvia pulled off her pinky-purple wig, revealing a head of silvery-grey hair.

"**Silver Shadow!**" Sprint gasped.

"Who else?" she said, walking into the workshop. "Bounce's inventions will make me a **FORTUNE!**"

49

5
A STRETCHY SOLUTION

"That crafty criminal," Sprint muttered. "I must get free."

One of the robot dog's paws had fallen off and was trapped under the net with him. Sprint grabbed it and used the sharp, metal claws to saw through the tough netting. Then he wriggled free.

"Now, how can I stop Silver Shadow?" he thought.

Sprint remembered the parcel in the workshop's hallway. He sneaked inside. Sprint could hear Silver Shadow crashing about as she searched for inventions to steal.

Tearing open the parcel, Sprint pulled out the sheet of **Super Stretchy Elastic**. It was clear, like plastic food wrap, only thicker, **stretchy** and **VERY STRONG**.

Sprint shot outside and stretched the **Super Stretchy Elastic** across the garden. He hung it between two trees. Then he ran back to the doorway.

"**Look out, Silver Shadow,**" Sprint yelled into the workshop. "There's another robot guard dog, and it's coming to get you!"

"We'll see about that!" snarled Silver Shadow, charging out into the garden with a big sack on her back. "You're not the only one who's good at running."

Silver Shadow didn't notice the sheet of **Super Stretchy Elastic** in her path. It was like running into a really strong trampoline. It **stretched** and then **SPRANG** back, **SHOOTING** Silver Shadow through the air. She landed in a heap.

Moments later, the police arrived with Professor Bounce.

"My intruder alarm called the police," Professor Bounce said to Sprint. "Thank you so much for saving my inventions."

"You've not seen the last of me!" Silver Shadow shrieked as the police led her away.

"I'm not so sure about that," replied Sprint. "I think you'll be doing a long **stretch** in prison!"

With that, he picked up the **Super Stretchy Elastic** and sprinted back to Hero Academy.

AFTER READING ACTIVITIES

QUICK QUIZ

See how fast you can answer these questions!
Look back at the story if you can't remember.

1) What does Ben need to collect from Professor Bounce's workshop?

2) How does Sylvia Shadow get into Professor Bounce's workshop?

3) What things does Sprint face as part of Professor Bounce's anti-intruder system?

THINK ABOUT IT!

What are Sprint's first impressions of Sylvia Shadow and how do they change by the end of the story?

IMAGINE IT

Spot the four differences between the pictures of Sprint.

Answers: 1) Super Stretchy Elastic;
2) she pushed the door in;
3) robot guard dog, nets.